Expecting: tracing the cord between us

Christina Loveless

BookLeaf Publishing

India | USA | UK

Presentation by *BookLeaf Publishing*

Web: www.bookleafpub.com

E-mail: info@bookleafpub.com

ISBN: 9789363313477

First edition 2024

To my beautiful, wonderful, most amazing children: you are an incredible blessing and I wouldn't trade you for the world. Whatever pain and suffering I experienced in bringing you into this world, I would go through it all over again so long as I have you.

To my husband: you have been the best partner, support person, friend, lover and co parent anyone could ever imagine or hope for. I'm so lucky and grateful you're mine. I love you. Very very.

To the first ob/gyn who delivered my baby: seriously, fuck you

ACKNOWLEDGEMENT

I wouldn't have been brave enough to tackle this project without my favorite Scorpio. Thanks Pam, I love you, boo.

PREFACE

My first and third pregnancies were completely different and yet the struggles were strangely similar. I was woefully unprepared, things did not go as expected and life was forever marked into "before" and "after". This collection has served as a catharsis and a powerful tool in my therapy in reconciling myself between what I wanted and what happened. In addition to those particularly painful events, there are countless other parenting struggles that are far too common and often hidden from view. Hopefully, this can shine a light into the dark places that come with post partum depression, anxiety, and even psychosis that someone else may be struggling with. Please, if you see yourself in these pages, seek help. This world is better with you in it.

Someday

There will be an end
To the tasks that seem endless
There will be a quiet
To the chatter that never seems to stop
There will be
No more diapers
No more bottles
No more sticky fingers constantly grasping
This is a season
Big love and big emotions
Little hands and little problems
Sweet moments and sour faces
High highs and low lows
Though it feels endless
All
Seasons
End.

Just a Bowl

Today my daughter dropped a glass
It didn't break
I told her to be more careful
Then she dropped a bowl
It didn't break
I told her to be more careful
She dropped another bowl
It shattered
Then I broke
It was just a bowl
Just a bowl I bought with a friend who is no
longer a friend
Just a bowl for a party with people who are no
longer in my life
Just a bowl that won a contest that led to so
many wonderful moments that are no longer
moments but memories
Just a bowl
Now I must pick up the pieces

Proud

My hands have held miracles grown in my body
and pushed out through sheer force of will
My heart walks around in separate bodies
My breasts have fed their tiny bodies, nourishing
them as they've grown day by day
My womb now sits idly by, anticipating a guest
who will never arrive
My feet carry me to many places, to catch an
errant child, to pound a second heartbeat into the
ground as I attempt to outrace my own thoughts
My mind has created a dozen different worlds,
planned a thousand meals, talked around a
million possibilities
My body has created and sustained life
And I am proud of it

Sweet Feral Child

There's no need to hurt others simply to feed
yourself
There's plenty of food to go around, to feed your
aching belly
Come, eat at my table, you're welcome to share
what is there
Come, sit with me, you don't have to change
Come, as you are
No one will harm you, so long as you do the
same
You don't need to hide your claws here
Just draw no blood
Come, dear one, there's no need to fear
No one will try to tame your wild spirit
You are safe here with me
You are safe here
You are safe
You are

Lullaby

My empty womb sings to me
At night, when I cannot sleep
I hear its strains through the haze of my sleep
aids
It beckons me to bring life
Despite my own reticence
Even though the time has passed
I have gone too far and can't reach back
It pains my soul to hear the song
I push it far, far away from me
But every night, I hear it once again

Mother's lament

A deep ache inside my chest cries out
Wordless
A longing deep within that cannot be sated
My weary soul drags behind my body
Searching
Endlessly
For the missing piece
If only I could understand
If only I could find what it longs for, needs
The lamentation is in an ancient tongue that I
have never studied or heard before
And still
I feel the heaviness, the pain, the sorrow in the
words
Speak to me, O Spirit
Speak that I might understand
Despite the fragile limitations of this body and
mind
Together we can find a spot of peace and rest

Value/Worth

These words should mean something to me
Because it should mean something to me
The silence inside echoes like an empty vault
Barren and devoid of all that might fill it
Mimicking the lack inside my body
The only bit of my identity is derived from the
ability to bear life
Am I less now that I cannot bear more?
Perhaps my desire to create springs forth from
the inability to procreate
Is my worth measured in dollars and cents?
Or production? Or any other measurement?
Or by the amount of love given or received?
Where does the value of a life lie?
And how much is mine worth?

Rejection

Rejection is a starving dog
Surviving on only scraps
Hiding under the broken table
Hoping to avoid being kicked
Often failing at all of these

Failing to avoid the kicks

Failing to hide the swollen belly that is never
filled

Failing to survive

Its ribs protrude
Its gums recede
Its hair falls out
Until only a shadow remains

Feral
Frightened
Famished

Willing to risk it all for the tiniest morsel

For everything is nothing anyway

Mommy/mama/mom/bruh

9

The small hands clutch for me
The small voice cries for me
The small eyes watch for me
The small heart beats for me

The big hands wave for me to go
The big voice calls for me to leave
The big eyes roll for me to stop talking
The big heart breaks my own

Once

Once, I prayed not to be pregnant, because I
wasn't ready
Once, I prayed for another chance, to become a
mother this time on my terms
Once, I prayed and prayed and prayed to have
more children, because I didn't want an only,
lonely child
Once, I prayed to ask why I was having more
when the last time nearly killed me

Expecting

I didn't expect to be born, my sister was here
first
I didn't expect to be pregnant at twenty, but he
left anyway
I didn't expect to get pregnant so fast when we
started trying for a baby
I didn't expect to suffer secondary infertility
I didn't expect to fail to get pregnant for two
years
I didn't expect to finally get pregnant after
giving up hope
I didn't expect to suffer from postpartum
psychosis
I didn't expect a surprise pregnancy post
vasectomy
I didn't expect to be in denial for months
I didn't expect to consider other options
I didn't expect to go into labor early
I didn't expect my hospital to be shut down
because of a fire
I didn't expect to have a baby in the nICU
I didn't expect to be kept away from him for
hours and then days
I didn't expect to find my way back to myself
after being so lost for so long
I didn't expect any of this while I was expecting,
so where's the book for that?

What I did

12

I started the day with a snuggle and a hug and "it will be ok"
I followed that up with picking out clothes and changing a diaper and putting things away
Then it was breakfast time for everyone except me
And out the door to get everyone where they need to be
I did a bunch of things no one else will notice or appreciate
But by all means tell me how mean I am because you can't stay up late

Star

13

In your eyes I see oceans and a universe of stars
From one end of eternity to the other
My soul longed for yours before I knew you
were mine
Time means nothing when home is forever
where you are
Each day we are together takes the sting out of
the time we were apart
Our heartbeats echo one chest to another
I never would have imagined how much it meant
to be your mother

Keep away

They took my baby from me
They put him in a box
They said I couldn't see him
Separated us with locks
I asked to see my baby
They told me that I could
But I must not touch him
Or hold him (but I should)
They told me to leave my baby
To go back to my room
To sleep and rest, then sleep some more
To heal my empty womb
I asked "where is my baby?
Why am I all alone?"
They told me he was safe
I could watch him on my phone
I cried to hold my baby
But no one was there to hear
The nurse must have left these pills for me
To take away my fear

Alone

15

I lay in silent agony in the room that should be
full of joy
I cry myself to sleep when I cannot see the point
It was not supposed to be like this
I wonder how it all went wrong
Since they have all left me, I can't help but be
alone

Keep it in

There's a endless font of rage that lives inside
these veins
A volcano that slumbers deep within
Be quiet they said, sit still
Smile like the pretty little girl you are
Cross your ankles, bat your eyes
Anger is not for you but sadness we can abide
The thing with volcanoes is they don't sleep
forever
And when it finally explodes you cannot put it
back inside

Birth plan

Rips and tears
Caught unawares
Water breaks
Body shakes
Knees buckle
White knuckles
Scream and shout
Baby's out
Extra stitch?
Useless bitch
Crystal clear
Get out of here
Taboo?
Fuck you

Sea monkey

18

A pain tears through my abdomen
A few days late
I think it might be, but it can't
It shouldn't
I couldn't
But there it is
A body
So bloody
So tiny
I flush the little sea monkey back out to the sea
Thank you for setting me free

Touch

You woke me in the morning with your hands in
my hair
You asked to read a story, where I was to be
your chair
You wanted a snuggle before you took a nap
You had to watch your cartoons while sitting in
my lap
You poked and prodded, pulled and pushed
My arms were pinched and my cheeks were
smushed
My darling, I cannot take another touch
I have simply had much too much

Journey

A generational curse of mothers to daughters
We can't understand each other
Where do you end and I begin?
The demarcations are fuzzy
The boundaries are ill-defined
From one to the next, we seek to be known
But we operate with colored glasses
The light is skewed towards what we already
think
Making assumptions
Refusing to admit we might be wrong
How do I keep from getting dragged into the
undertow?
When this is all I've ever known?
I plant my feet and take a stand
I draw my line in the sand
I will not be washed away like so many shells
along the shore
I wrap myself in kelp and hold tight to the little
hands I anchor
I keep my eyes above the tide and drift along
with the current
So long as I can be by their side
This journey is always worth it

Catharsis

There was a dream
Where I was alone
The light was soft
It felt like home
But it was quiet
And far too still
I can't go back
I never will
I used to think all that I wanted was to make you
proud
I'm so glad I realized that I do deserve to be
happy and that those who truly love me will
never ask me to put myself in a box
I don't need to cut off bits and pieces to fit neatly
inside your lines
I love my life without you in it
Isn't that a surprise?